Tigers

ABDO
Publishing Company

A Buddy Book
by
Julie Murray

VISIT US AT
www.abdopub.com

Published by Buddy Books, an imprint of ABDO Publishing Company, 4940 Viking Drive, Suite 622, Edina, Minnesota 55435. Copyright © 2002 by Abdo Consulting Group, Inc. International copyrights reserved in all countries. No part of this book may be reproduced in any form without written permission from the publisher.

Printed in the United States.

Edited by: Christy DeVillier
Contributing Editors: Matt Ray, Michael P. Goecke
Graphic Design: Maria Hosley
Image Research: Deborah Coldiron
Cover Photograph: Digital Stock Corp.
Interior Photographs: Digital Stock Corp., Digital Vision Ltd., Eyewire Inc., Getty Images

Library of Congress Cataloging-in-Publication Data

Murray, Julie, 1969-
　　Tigers/Julie Murray.
　　　　p. cm. — (Animal kingdom)
　　Summary: A simple description of the habitat, physical characteristics, life cycle, and eating habits of tigers, the biggest of the big cats.
　　ISBN 1-57765-646-6
　　　　1. Tigers—Juvenile literature. [1. Tigers.] I. Title. II. Animal kingdom (Edina, Minn.)

QL737.C23 M9 2002
599.756—dc21

2001046119

Contents

The Biggest Cat

Tigers are the biggest cats in the world. Leopards, jaguars, and lions are big cats, too.

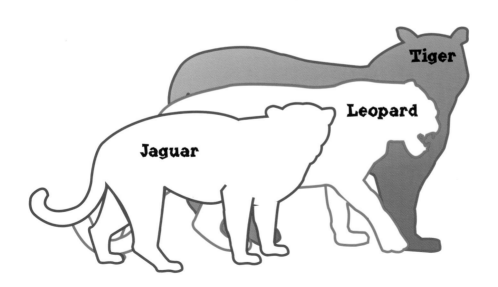

Tiger

Leopard

Jaguar

What makes these big cats different from other cats? Have you ever heard a house cat roar? Only tigers, leopards, jaguars, and lions can roar. Also, most big cats eat while lying down. Does a house cat eat like a tiger? No, house cats sit or stand to eat.

What They Look Like

Tigers are huge. Most tigers grow over 10 feet (3 m) long. A Sumatran male tiger weighs about 250 pounds (113 kg). A Siberian male tiger can weigh over 500 pounds (226 kg). The heaviest tiger on record is a 1,025-pound (465-kg) Siberian male.

Tigers are the biggest cats.

Most tigers are orange with black stripes. These colors and marks match the tiger's land. This helps tigers catch **prey**.

Where They Live

Tigers can live in many different **habitats**. These cats live in jungles, forests, mountains, and grasslands. A tiger's habitat must have hiding places like trees or tall grasses. Plenty of **prey** and water are important, too.

Tigers live in places with trees or tall grasses.

Tigers can live in cold, snowy places, too.

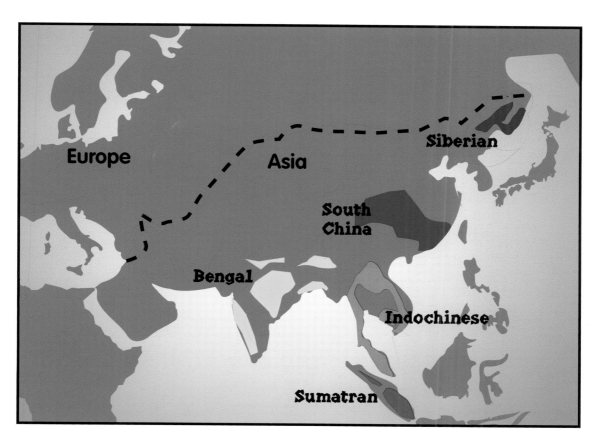

KIND OF TIGER	WHERE IT LIVES
Siberian	Southeastern Russia
South China	Southern China
Bengal	India
Sumatran	Sumatra
Indochinese	Southeast Asia

No More Tigers?

Caspian, Javan, and Balinese tigers are not around anymore. These tigers are **extinct**. There is a chance that today's tigers may die out, too. People are killing tigers and destroying their **habitats**.

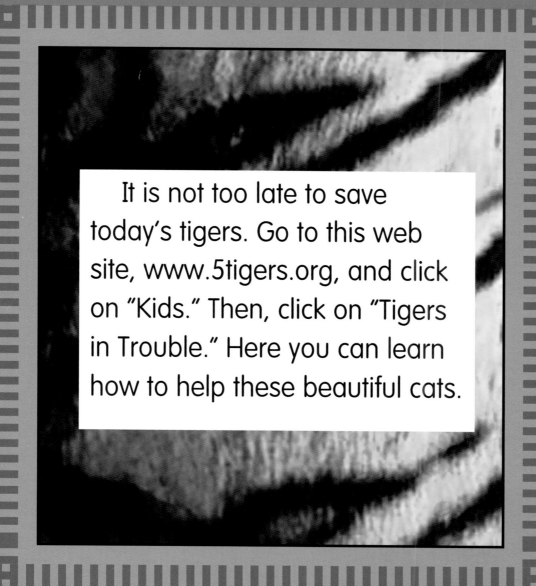

It is not too late to save today's tigers. Go to this web site, www.5tigers.org, and click on "Kids." Then, click on "Tigers in Trouble." Here you can learn how to help these beautiful cats.

Hunting And Eating

Like all wild cats, tigers are good hunters. They use their sharp teeth and claws to catch and eat animals. These **carnivores** hunt deer, wild pigs, young elephants, and rhinos. Tigers also eat fish, lizards, monkeys, birds, snakes, and rats. A wild tiger will eat about 40 pounds (18 kg) of food at one time. After eating a big meal, a tiger can go without food for days.

Tigers are good hunters.

Territories

A **territory** is a tiger's hunting land. A territory must have enough **prey** to feed the tiger. Tigers need big territories when few prey are around. A tiger's territory can be as big as 120 square miles (311 sq km).

Tigers mark their **territories**. Tigers mark by scratching trees and leaving their smells. These marks tell other male tigers to stay away. But a male tiger commonly allows a tigress, or female tiger, to live nearby.

Swimming Cats

Tigers are cats that love water. A tiger may spend much of its day cooling off in water. These big cats will swim in streams or rivers, too. Some tigers can swim more than three miles (four km) at a time.

Tigers are good swimmers.

Tiger Cubs

A tigress finds a hidden **den** to have her babies. This den helps to keep tiger babies, or cubs, safe. A mother tigress commonly raises two or three cubs at one time.

A newborn tiger cub is blind. After about two weeks, a cub can see. After about eight weeks, cubs begin eating meat.

Tiger cubs are born blind and helpless.

Cubs learn to hunt from their mothers. Around age two, tigers can hunt for themselves. At this time, an adult tiger leaves its mother. An adult tiger may live another 13 years in the wild.

Important Words

carnivore meat-eater.

den a hiding place for tiger cubs.

extinct when all members of a certain animal no longer exist, or live.

habitat where an animal lives in the wild.

prey an animal that is food for another animal.

territory an area of land to live and hunt upon.

Web Sites

5 Tigers:
The Tiger Information Center

www.5tigers.org/
A special section for kids includes games, facts, and ways to help save tigers from extinction.

Tiger Territory

www.lairweb.org.nz/tiger/
Packed with information, this site is a great source for tiger facts.

Cyber Tiger

www.nationalgeographic.com/
tigers/maina.html
You are the zookeeper in this fun game that teaches about tigers.

Index